# Meaning
# *Matters*

## Vocabulary

*Finding Meaning
Beyond Words*

— Linda Kita-Bradley —

Grass Roots Press

Meaning Matters: Vocabulary
© 2019 Grass Roots Press
www.grassrootsbooks.net

Grass Roots Press acknowledges the financial support
of the Government of Canada for our publishing activities.

Produced with the assistance of the Government of Alberta.

Canada   Alberta
          Government

Editor: Dr. Pat Campbell
Image Research: Linda Kita-Bradley

**Library and Archives Canada Cataloguing in Publication**

Kita-Bradley, Linda, 1958–, author
    Vocabulary / Linda Kita-Bradley.

(Meaning matters)
ISBN 978-1-77153-234-1 (softcover)

    1. Vocabulary—Problems, exercises, etc.  2. English language—
Problems, exercises, etc.  I. Title.

PE1449.K58 2018        428.1        C2018-901992-1

Printed in Canada

# Contents

# Unit 1: Context Clues

As a reader you will always encounter new and difficult words. How do you respond when you come across a word you don't know? Do you stop or do you continue to read? Do you reach for a dictionary?

Defining difficult words is a challenge, especially if you don't have a dictionary. Writers help the reader by including context clues in their writing.

## What are context clues?

A context clue is information in a sentence or paragraph that helps you define a difficult word. In the sentence below, you can use context clues to make a logical guess about the meaning of **lethargic**.

Larry was **lethargic** and didn't have the energy to get out of bed.

The writer tells you Larry has no energy. You can use this information to make a logical guess or inference about how Larry feels. Larry feels too tired to get out of bed. **Lethargic** must mean lacking energy and tired.

## Be a Detective

*Search for the Clues*

Pause and pronounce the difficult word.

Re-read the sentence or paragraph.

Look for context clues.

Use the clues to make a logical guess as to the meaning of the word.

## Types of Context Clues

Look at the different types of context clues below. Discuss with your teacher how the context clues help you figure out the meanings of the new words.

| Type of Context Clue | Description | Example |
|---|---|---|
| Definition | The writer provides a definition of the word. | A food allergy can cause **anaphylaxis**—<u>a serious reaction to an allergy</u>. |
| Synonym | The sentence or paragraph contains a word or phrase that means the same as the target word. | It is **essential** to read all food labels carefully. It is also <u>important</u> to ask questions about the food you eat in restaurants. |
| Antonym | The sentence or paragraph contains a word or phrase that means the opposite of the target word. | Some symptoms like runny nose are <u>not too serious</u>, but some symptoms like a fast heartbeat and trouble breathing can be **severe**. |
| Examples | The meaning has to be figured out or inferred from the information or examples in the text. | A food allergy can cause **symptoms** such as <u>a runny nose</u>, <u>skin rash</u>, and <u>sneezing</u>. |

Using context clues will help to expand your vocabulary.

Sometimes using context clues will not give you the *exact* meanings of new words, but you will be able to figure out the *general* meanings of new words.

You are going to read about earthquakes.
Use context clues to figure out the meanings of the bolded words.
Underline the context clue(s) that helped you figure out the meaning.

## Example:

The earth's crust is made of tectonic plates that are always moving. Every once in a while two grinding plates will suddenly **jolt** into a new position. This <u>sudden movement</u> sends shock waves that radiate through rock, soil, buildings, and water. The energy released by this <u>abrupt movement</u> creates an earthquake.

**Context clues help you figure out that the meaning of *jolt* is a sudden or abrupt movement.**

❶ The Richter **magnitude** scale is used to describe the strength of an earthquake. An earthquake that measures 7.0 on the Richter scale can destroy buildings.

Choose the word that means the same as **magnitude**.

A. sound        B. location        C. depth        D. size

Underline the context clues that helped you figure out the meaning.

❷ Some earthquakes consist of small tremors that cause little damage. Other earthquakes are so **massive** that they destroy whole cities.

Choose the word that means the same as **massive**.

A. little        B. hidden        C. large        D. quick

Underline the context clues that helped you figure out the meaning.

❸ Earthquakes **impact** people in many ways. They cause injury and loss of life as well as damage to roads, bridges, and buildings.

Choose the word that means the same as **impact**.

A. affect        B. help        C. move        D. change

Underline the context clues that helped you figure out the meaning.

④ Floods, fires, gas leaks, and landslides are possible **consequences** of an earthquake.

Choose the word that means the same as **consequences**.

A. causes  B. movements  C. uses  D. results

Underline the context clues that helped you figure out the meaning.

⑤ Earthquakes cause the most damage in places like big cities. If these **populated** places are near the sea, damage is not only worse. It causes death.

Choose the phrase that means the same as **populated**.

A. having lots of earthquakes  B. having lots of floods
C. having lots of people  D. having lots of crime

Underline the context clues that helped you figure out the meaning.

⑥ Earthquakes can cause **enormous** ocean waves as tall as buildings. These huge waves crash into cities along the coast.

Choose the phrase that means the same as **enormous**.

A. very salty  B. very loud  C. very slow  D. very big

Underline the context clues that helped you figure out the meaning.

⑦ Scientists can **predict** that an earthquake will happen in the future, but they cannot tell when exactly the earthquake will happen.

Choose the phrase that means the same as **predict**.

A. say in advance  B. plan in advance  C. be afraid  D. make sure

Underline the context clues that helped you figure out the meaning.

Which *types* of context clues did you find in questions 1 to 7?

**You are going to read about wildfires.**
**Use context clues to figure out the meanings of the bolded words.**

## Paragraph 1: What Causes a Wildfire?

Wildfires are fires that are out of control. An unattended campfire or a discarded cigarette butt can ignite a wildfire. Hot weather, lightning, or the sun's heat can start a wildfire. Dry **vegetation** such as grass and bushes act as fuel for a fire. And wind can aid a wildfire's progress. Wildfires can burn large areas of land and destroy everything in their paths in minutes.

❶ Choose the word that means the same as **vegetation**.

A. shrubs       B. farmland       C. forests       D. plants

❷ Underline the context clues that helped you figure out the meaning.

## Paragraph 2: The Fort McMurray Wildfire

On May 1, 2016, a wildfire began in Fort McMurray, Alberta. Nature was not on the firefighters' side. High temperatures were at record levels that week. The rains would not come. The strong winds would not die down. The fire **escalated** and rapidly increased in size, spreading over one million acres in three weeks. In mid-June, rain and cool temperatures helped firefighters control the fire.

❶ What do you think **escalated** means? Write the meaning in the space below.

........................................................................................................................................................

❷ Underline the context clues that helped you figure out the meaning.

❸ Check the new word's exact meaning in the Answer Key. Is your meaning close to the exact meaning? In what ways are the two meanings similar?

Which *types* of context clues did you find in the paragraphs on this page?

**You are going to read about avalanches.**
**Use context clues to figure out the meanings of the bolded words.**

## Paragraph 1: What Causes an Avalanche?

With every snowfall, another layer of snow **accumulates** on a mountain. Some layers are strong; other layers are weak and unstable. The weight of another snowfall can cause a weak layer to dislodge. The weak layer starts to slide down the mountain, pulling more layers of snow with it. The snow speeds up until it is moving as fast as a vehicle speeding down a highway.

❶ Choose the word that means the same as **accumulates**.

A. melts          B. collects          C. disappears          D. sticks

❷ Underline the context clues that helped you figure out the meaning.

## Paragraph 2: Avalanche Disaster

An earthquake shook the coast of Peru. Then it shook the mountains of Peru. A huge piece of glacier high in the mountains broke away. The glacier became part of an avalanche made up of ice, rock, and mud. The avalanche crashed down the mountain at speeds of up to 160 kilometres per hour. It covered more than 17 kilometres. It buried two towns under 100 metres of **debris**.

❶ What do you think **debris** means? Write the meaning in the space below.

...............................................................................................................................................

❷ Underline the context clues that helped you figure out the meaning.

❸ Check the new word's exact meaning in the Answer Key. Is your meaning close to the exact meaning? In what ways are the two meanings similar?

Which *types* of context clues did you find in the paragraphs on this page?

**You are going to read about hurricanes.**
**Use context clues to figure out the meanings of the bolded words.**

## Paragraph 1: How Do Hurricanes Form?

Hurricanes form over warm ocean water near the equator. Each hurricane follows a similar **cycle** of development. The series of events begins when the warm moist air rises. The rising air creates an area of low pressure. Air from the surrounding area rushes in to the low-pressure area. This process keeps happening until a large mass of warm, moist air with rain clouds is formed over the ocean. The winds and clouds begin to spin in a huge circle, and a hurricane is born.

❶ Choose the phrase that means the same as **cycle**.

A. the development of an event　　　B. the development of a natural disaster
C. a set of events　　　D. a set of events that happens in the same order

❷ Underline the context clues that helped you figure out the meaning.

## Paragraph 2: Hurricane Katrina

On August 29, 2005, Hurricane Katrina struck the Gulf Coast of the United States. More than 1,200 people died. In addition to the death toll, one million people lost their homes. But not only people suffered. Beaches were lost to floods caused by the high seas. The floods caused **erosion**—the wearing away of land. Sea animals, birds, and turtles had now lost the grounds where they once raised their young.

❶ What do you think **erosion** means? Write the meaning in the space below.

.............................................................................................................................................

❷ Underline the context clues that helped you figure out the meaning.

❸ Check the new word's exact meaning in the Answer Key. Is your meaning close to the exact meaning? In what ways are the two meanings similar?

Which *types* of context clues did you find in the paragraphs on this page?

# Unit 2: Metaphors *and* Similes

**Which sentence do you find more interesting?**

*She is smart* or *She is as sharp as a tack*?

Writers use metaphors and similes to express ideas in interesting ways.
Metaphors and similes help people to form a vivid picture of what they are reading.

*What is a metaphor?*

A metaphor is a figure of speech that compares one thing to another.

Look at the following example:

The *future* will be nothing but *clear skies*.

In this metaphor, the writer compares the future to clear skies. Clear skies mean no clouds and sunny days. The writer implies that the future is going to be good. There will be happy days and no problems.

*What is a simile?*

A simile is a figure of speech that compares two things using the words *like* or *as*.

Look at the following examples:

The moon hung low in the sky *like* a pumpkin.
The moon hung low in the sky *as* big and fat *as* a pumpkin.

In these similes, the moon is compared to a pumpkin. The moon looks big and fat.
What colour do you think the moon is? If you said orange, you are right.

## Give It a Try

Look at the following examples. Identify two metaphors and two similes.
Discuss with your teacher what is being compared and what the writer is trying to say.

1. The fog was as thick as pea soup.
2. Life is a rollercoaster.
3. Watching the show was like watching the grass grow.
4. The computer in the classroom was a dinosaur.

**Read the following metaphors.**
**Identify the two things being compared.**
**Choose the best answer for what the writer is trying to say.**
**Give reasons for your choices.**

❶  The wind was a knife cutting through me.

A. What is being compared? _____ and _____

B. Which sentence best matches what the writer wants to say?

(i) The wind made me bleed.            (ii) The wind was very cold.
(iii) The wind suddenly stopped.       (iv) The wind was gentle.

Give a reason for your choice.

❷  The ocean was a tank of boiling water.

A. What is being compared? _____ and _____

B. Which sentence best matches what the writer wants to say?

(i) The ocean was huge.               (ii) The ocean was clear.
(iii) The ocean was salty.            (iv) The ocean was rough.

Give a reason for your choice.

❸  My head is filled with a storm of ideas.

A. What is being compared? _____ and _____

B. Which sentence best matches what the writer wants to say?

(i) I have a lot of ideas            (ii) I have really good ideas.
(iii) I have clear ideas.            (iv) I have a lot of ideas about storms.

Give a reason for your choice.

**Read the following metaphors.**
**Identify the two things being compared.**
**Figure out what the writer is trying to say.**

④ My childhood memories are a fog.

A. What is being compared? _____ and _____

B. What words come to mind when you think of fog?

.................................................................................................................................

C. What does the comparison suggest about the childhood memories?

The childhood memories.............................................................................................. .

⑤ Her daughter is the sunshine of her life.

A. What is being compared? _____ and _____

B. What words come to mind when you think of sunshine?

.................................................................................................................................

C. What does the comparison suggest about her daughter?

The daughter ................................................................................................................. .

⑥ The flooding river was a hungry mouth eating the land.

A. What is being compared? _____ and _____

B. What words come to mind when you think of a hungry mouth?

.................................................................................................................................

C. What does the comparison suggest about the flooding river?

The flooding river ......................................................................................................... .

**Read each sentence.**
**Choose the metaphor that best matches the meaning of the sentence.**
**Give a reason for your choice.**

❶  This homework is so easy.

   A. This homework is a gusty day.

   B. This homework is a breeze.

   C. This homework is a hurricane.

❷  The boss was really mad when he came into the room.

   A. The boss thundered into the room.

   B. The boss breezed into the room.

   C. The boss melted when he came into the room.

❸  I'm very, very old.

   A. I'm at the dawn of my life.

   B. I'm in the autumn of my life.

   C. I'm in the sunset years of my life.

❹  Things are not looking so good for him right now.

   A. Into each life some rain must fall.

   B. He is going to experience a blizzard of activity.

   C. Grey skies are going to clear up.

❺  She gave him a lot of gifts.

   A. Gift-giving was suffering a drought.

   B. She was a gift of sunshine to him.

   C. She showered him with gifts.

**Read the following similes.**
**Identify what two things are being compared.**
**Choose the best answer for what the writer is trying to say.**
**Give reasons for your choices.**

**❶** The sun felt as warm as toast.

   A. What is being compared? _____ and _____

   B. Which sentence best matches what the writer wants to say?

   (i) The sun was yellow.                (ii) The sun was gentle.
   (iii) The sun was bright.              (iv) The sun was burning.

   Give a reason for your choice.

**❷** The clouds looked like cotton candy.

   A. What is being compared? _____ and _____

   B. Which sentence best matches what the writer wants to say?

   (i) The clouds looked fluffy.          (ii) The clouds looked like cloth.
   (iii) The clouds looked dark.          (iv) The clouds looked sticky.

   Give a reason for your choice.

**❸** The hot summer days weighed us down like a wet blanket.

   A. What is being compared? _____ and _____

   B. Which sentence best matches what the writer wants to say?

   (i) The days were bright.              (ii) The days were long.
   (iii) The days were humid.             (iv) The days were stormy.

   Give a reason for your choice.

**Read the following similes.**
**Identify the two things being compared.**
**Figure out what the writer is trying to say.**

④ Walking on the frosty sidewalks was like walking on ice.

   A. What is being compared? _____ and _____

   B. What words come to mind when you think of ice?

   .............................................................................................................................................

   C. What does the comparison suggest about the sidewalks?

   The sidewalks............................................................................................................. .

⑤ Shoveling through the snowdrifts was as fun as eating dirt.

   A. What is being compared? _____ and _____

   B. What words come to mind when you think of eating dirt?

   .............................................................................................................................................

   C. What does the comparison suggest about shoveling snowdrifts?

   Shoveling snowdrifts ................................................................................................ .

⑥ The wind was as playful as a kitten.

   A. What is being compared? _____ and _____

   B. What words come to mind when you think of a kitten playing?

   .............................................................................................................................................

   C. What does the comparison suggest about the wind?

   The wind .................................................................................................................... .

**Read each sentence.**
**Choose the simile that *you think* best matches the meaning of the sentence.**
**Give a reason for your choice.**

❶ She pretended to smile.

    A. Her smile was as warm as sunshine.

    B. Her smile was as sad as a country song.

    C. Her smile was as stiff as an icicle.

❷ He cried and cried and cried.

    A. His tears were like drops of dew on the grass.

    B. His tears were like a summer shower.

    C. His tears were like a cloudburst.

❸ She likes to wear brightly-coloured clothes.

    A. Her clothes are as fresh as a spring day.

    B. Her clothes are as bright as a full moon.

    C. Her clothes are as colourful as a rainbow.

❹ He stopped smiling when he saw his daughter.

    A. His face lit up like the sun.

    B. His face darkened like a black cloud.

    C. His face softened like a misty rain.

❺ She worries too much.

    A. Her thoughts are as heavy as wet snow.

    B. Her thoughts float like falling leaves.

    C. Her thoughts are as wild as waves in a stormy sea.

Idioms are a natural part of speech—they add colour and interest to a language. Often, people fail to realize they are using idioms. Learning idioms is like learning another language. Learning idioms can be challenging, even confusing, but they are fun to learn!

## What is an idiom?

An idiom is a phrase, or a group of words, that has a special meaning. To determine the meaning of an idiom, you need to look at the entire phrase. You cannot just look at the meaning of each word in the idiom. You have to think about how the idiom is used in the context of a sentence or paragraph.

*Stay on the ball* is an idiom. In your mind, visualize what staying on a ball might look like. Does the idiom mean that we want somebody to balance on a large ball? Probably not. Read the idiom in the paragraph. Use the context clues to figure out the meaning of *stay on the ball*.

> **Stay on the ball** throughout your entire shift at work. If you don't, you might start making mistakes. Make sure to arrive at work feeling alert and full of energy. Rather than multi-tasking, try to dedicate your attention to one task at a time. Avoid distractions that take you away from your task.

Did you figure out that *staying on the ball* means paying attention or concentrating?

If yes, you are right. How can you remember the meaning? One way to remember the meaning of new idioms is to relate them to your experiences.

## Give It a Try

**Read the following paragraph.**
**Discuss with your teacher the meaning of the idiom.**

> I was extremely busy at work this week because we needed to process several large orders. Today, I realized that I had mixed up two orders. Naturally, the customers were angry. I spent a lot of time sorting out that mix-up. I really **dropped the ball** on those orders, but at least the customers are satisfied.

Describe a time when you **dropped the ball**.

**Read each paragraph.**
**Choose the best meaning for the idiom.**
**Write a sentence using the idiom.**

① Finding a decent job requires hard work and dedication. In many cases, it involves some luck, too. One method of **getting your foot in the door** is to accept a lower- paying job. Then you need to do your best at the job at every opportunity. And who knows? The lower-paying job might result in a higher-paying job.

A. paying your bills
C. avoiding hard work

B. causing pain
D. getting a chance at something

How can volunteering help people **get their foot in the door** to find a job? Use *get a foot in the door* in a sentence.

..................................................................................................................................

② Job interviews provide you with the opportunity to **start off on the right foot**. Put some thought into how you dress. Stains on your outfit leave a negative impression. Choose clean street shoes over running shoes, sandals, or flip-flops. Wear socks or stockings. Leave cool hats, chunky jewellery, and piercings at home.

A. start with your strong leg
C. start a new job

B. start off first
D. start in a positive way

Why is it important to **start off on the right foot**? Use *start off on the right foot* in a sentence.

..................................................................................................................................

③ In many cases, starting a new job means meeting new people. Meeting new people can be stressful. Start by shaking hands firmly, making eye contact, and saying your name confidently. Smiling is always a good start to **breaking the ice** with strangers.

A. solving problems
C. learning names

B. having a cold drink
D. making people feel relaxed

Are you good at **breaking the ice**? Use *breaking the ice* in a sentence.

..................................................................................................................................

④ Training for a new job means learning a lot in a short time. Ask the trainer to repeat information when necessary. Do not be afraid to ask questions. Asking questions shows the trainer that you want to learn. **Learning the ropes** on a new job is your responsibility as well as the trainer's.

A. learning what to say      B. learning the basics of something
C. learning how to listen      D. learning how to tie knots

When was the last time you had to **learn the ropes**?
Use *learn the ropes* in a sentence.

......................................................................................................

......................................................................................................

⑤ Working with other people may lead to conflict at times. Conflict is okay. People do not always have to **see eye to eye**. People can disagree or have different opinions. However, it is important to know how to deal with conflict.

A. deal with each other      B. agree with each other
C. look at each other      D. argue with each other

Is there someone you don't **see eye to eye** with?
Use *see eye to eye* in a sentence.

......................................................................................................

......................................................................................................

⑥ Following rules in the workplace is important. However, rules sometimes do not work in certain situations. Or in some situations, there are no rules to follow. In those cases, you will have to **think outside the box**.

A. follow just the important rules      B. choose another box
C. go outside and think      D. think of a new solution

Think of words that describe people who **think outside the box**.
Use *think outside the box* in a sentence.

......................................................................................................

......................................................................................................

**7** When you are in a hurry, **cutting corners** is tempting. For example, you're behind schedule, so you throw broken glass into a garbage bag. But you're supposed to put broken glass in a plastic container. Later, you grab the garbage bag and cut your hand.

A. breaking rules to save time
C. hurting oneself to get time off work

B. turning a corner
D. forgetting the rules

When do you **cut corners**?
Use *cut corners* in a sentence.

........................................................................................................

........................................................................................................

**8** Nobody likes a complainer, but sometimes you need to complain. For example, if your boss refuses to pay overtime, you need to speak out. Your boss might not like it, and he may even give you a hard time. However, **rocking the boat** in this case is the right decision.

A. doing something to disrupt a situation
C. not liking your boss

B. working too hard
D. taking action to make somebody angry

What would cause you to **rock the boat** at a workplace?
Use *rock the boat* in a sentence.

........................................................................................................

........................................................................................................

**9** Cell phones are a marvelous invention, but they are not so great on the job. When the phone rings, it's a **safe bet** you will be tempted to answer it right away. Turn your phone off, and tell friends and family you won't respond to personal calls at work.

A. something that will lose money
C. something that will probably happen

B. something that is not dangerous
D. something that is new

Is it a **safe bet** that you will never lose your cell phone?
Use *safe bet* in a sentence.

........................................................................................................

........................................................................................................

**Read each paragraph.**
**Figure out the meaning of the idiom.**
**Write a sentence using the idiom.**

❶ Do you ever feel **snowed under** at work? Do you feel you will never complete your work on schedule? Do you feel under pressure constantly? Try dealing with simple tasks immediately. Don't let simple tasks accumulate, because they can become one huge job that never gets done.

A. What do you think *snowed under* means? Write a definition.

.............................................................................................................................................

B. Write a sentence using *snowed under*.

.............................................................................................................................................

❷ Offer to perform little tasks at work before being asked. Clean the coffeepot in the lunchroom, or help set up seating for a meeting. Doing little tasks like these shows your boss that you willingly **go the extra mile**.

A. What do you think *go the extra mile* means? Write a definition.

.............................................................................................................................................

B. Write a sentence using *go the extra mile*.

.............................................................................................................................................

❸ Don't **bite off more than you can chew** at work. Working hard and volunteering to do extra tasks is appreciated by others, but don't feel pressured to do everything. Let somebody else clean the microwave. Doing too much can be stressful.

A. What do you think *bite off more than you can chew* means? Write a definition.

.............................................................................................................................................

B. Write a sentence using *bite off more than you can chew*.

.............................................................................................................................................

④ Do you ever have trouble knowing who is **calling the shots** at work? The boss says you need to do this, but the supervisor says you need to do that. Then a co-worker tells you something different. Find out who is responsible for making decisions.

A. What do you think *calling the shots* means? Write a definition.

....................................................................................................................................

B. Write a sentence using *calling the shots*.

....................................................................................................................................

⑤ Who your co-workers are and who you answer to at work can alter quickly. Employees get fired and new people get hired. Co-workers change jobs, and supervisors come and go. Don't **burn bridges**. Work at maintaining a good relationship with everyone.

A. What do you think *burn bridges* means? Write a definition.

....................................................................................................................................

B. Write a sentence using *burn bridges*.

....................................................................................................................................

⑥ The workplace can be full of rumours. Focus on your work and **keep your head down**. Walk away when people start gossiping about co-workers or their bosses. Don't say negative things about others, and above all, don't choose sides in conflicts.

A. What do you think *keep your head down* means? Write a definition.

....................................................................................................................................

B. Write a sentence using *keep your head down*.

....................................................................................................................................

# Unit 4: Dictionary

Fluent readers use dictionaries and context clues to figure out the meaning of new words. Looking up every new word you see or hear takes too much time. So, begin by using context clues to help you figure out the meaning. If that doesn't work, turn to the dictionary.

## What is the benefit of using a dictionary?

A dictionary gives the definition of words. But that's not all. Look at the dictionary entry below. What other information does a dictionary provide?

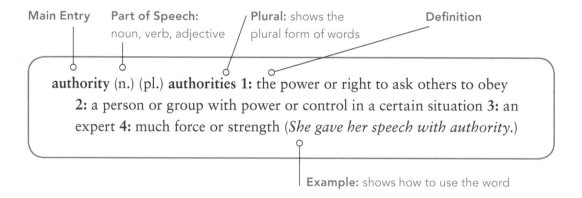

Main Entry
Part of Speech: noun, verb, adjective
Plural: shows the plural form of words
Definition

**authority** (n.) (pl.) **authorities 1:** the power or right to ask others to obey **2:** a person or group with power or control in a certain situation **3:** an expert **4:** much force or strength (*She gave her speech with authority.*)

**Example:** shows how to use the word

**Use the dictionary entry for *authority* to answer the following questions:**

❶ How many definitions for *authority* are in the dictionary entry? _____

❷ Circle the part of speech for *authority*.   noun (n.)   verb (v.)   adjective (adj.)

❸ Circle the correct spelling for the plural of authority.

   A. authoritys          B. authoriteys          C. authorities          D. authoritis

❹ What does *authority* mean in the sentence below?

   She gave her speech with **authority**. The word *authority* means _____.

**Use the dictionary entries to answer the questions.**

> **cause** (n.) **1:** a person or thing that produces an effect or makes something happen (*Heavy rain was the cause of the flooding.*) **2:** a reason (*I have no cause to complain.*) **3:** a belief or purpose that is supported (*He gave money to the cause of animal rights.*)
>
> **cause** (v.) **1:** to be the reason for something happening (*The drunk driver caused the accident.*) **2:** to make happen (*His happiness caused me to smile.*)

❶ Complete the sentence: The word *cause* is a noun and a _____.

❷ How many definitions for *cause* as a noun are in the dictionary entry? _____

❸ How many examples do the dictionary entries give for *cause*? _____

The dictionary entries for *cause* do not show the plural form. This is because the plural form is easy to spell. Just add s—causes.

> **valid** (adj.) **1:** having reason and sense (*His excuse for being late for work is not valid.*) **2:** acceptable in law **3:** within an expiry date (*The coupon is valid until the end of the month.*)

❹ How many definitions for *valid* are in the dictionary entry? _____

❺ Circle the part of speech for *valid*: noun (n.)   verb (v.)   adjective (adj.)

❻ Underline the first example for *valid*. What do you think his excuse was?

❼ Why does the dictionary entry not show a plural form for *valid*?

## One Word—Many Meanings

The main reason we use a dictionary is to find definitions of words. Many words have more than one definition. Look at the two dictionary entries for the word *source* below. The first entry provides five definitions for *source* as a noun (n.); the second entry provides two definitions for *source* as a verb (v.).

*Exercise 1*

**Read the sentences below.**
**Use the dictionary entries to find the definition of *source* in each sentence.**

**The first one is an example.**

① People use the Internet to **source** all types of information. v. 1

② The **source** of the Mackenzie River is Great Slave Lake. _____

③ The reporter's **source** wanted to stay nameless. _____

④ Chocolate companies **source** cocoa beans from West Africa. _____

⑤ High drug use is a **source** of concern for city council. _____

⑥ Old newspapers provide an interesting **source** of historical facts. _____

⑦ Deep green, leafy vegetables are a good **source** of iron. _____

⑧ My children are a **source** of joy to me. _____

---

**source** (n.) **1:** a person, place or thing from which something starts or from which you can get something (*The sun is a source of Vitamin D.*) **2:** a cause of or reason for (*Her bad marks were a source of worry for her mother.*) **3:** a book or document that has original information or evidence (*Her diary is a source of old-time recipes.*) **4:** a person who gives information **5:** the beginning place of a river or stream

**source** (v.) **1:** to find out where you can get something (*It's a good idea to source health advice carefully.*) **2:** to get from a certain place (*The company sources coffee beans from Brazil.*)

---

## Exercise 2

**Read the sentences below.**

**Use the dictionary entries to find the definition of *separate* in each sentence.**

**The first one is an example.**

❶ She has to keep her cats in **separate** rooms because they fight.  <u>adj. 3</u>

❷ The friends **separate** at the lights because they go to different schools. _____

❸ Railway tracks **separate** the downtown. _____

❹ They had to **separate** after only two years of marriage. _____

❺ They **separated** the clothes into two piles: men's and women's. _____

❻ A row of trees **separates** our yard from the neighbour's yard. _____

❼ I bought the scarf as a **separate**. _____

❽ The restaurant area is **separate** from the bar. _____

❾ Keep your bus ticket **separate** so you can find it quickly. _____

❿ **Separate** the sick girl from the other students so that she doesn't spread germs. _____

---

**separate** (adj.) **1:** apart from other things or by itself (*Batteries are not included; they are separate.*) **2:** not joined or touching (*The family bathroom is separate from the women's.*) **3:** not the same (*Keep raw meat and vegetables in separate bowls.*)

**separate** (n.) a piece of clothing that is worn with other matching pieces of clothing (*She bought separates, a blouse and skirt, instead of a dress.*)

**separate** (v.) **1:** to move a thing or things and set apart (*You should separate a rotten apple from the rest of the apples.*) **2:** to divide things into groups (*Separate the garbage into paper, cans, bottles and plastics.*) **3:** to go different ways (*They separated when they reached the main street.*) **4:** to cut into two parts (*The canal separates the city.*) **5:** to form a boundary (*A white line separates the bike lane from the traffic.*) **6:** to stop living together as a married couple

## Exercise 3

**Read the sentences below.**
**Use the dictionary entries to find the definition of *review* in each sentence.**

**The first one is an example.**

① My boss does a work **review** once a year.  n. 1

② It's a good idea to **review** material soon after you learn it. _____

③ In December, news shows often do a **review** of that year's top stories. _____

④ Heads of state often **review** troops while visiting other countries. _____

⑤ She **reviewed** her answers before handing in the exam. _____

⑥ Many technology critics gave the new device negative **reviews**. _____

⑦ The teacher handed out a **review** of math formulas we should know. _____

⑧ The police finally arrived to **review** the crime scene. _____

⑨ Imagine being paid to spend your time watching and **reviewing** movies. _____

⑩ A political speech goes through many **reviews** before anyone hears it. _____

**review** (n.) **1:** general assessment of something **2:** the act of looking at something to make changes or improvements **3:** report that gives an opinion about a new book, movie, or product **4:** the act of visiting and looking at military groups by an important person **5:** summary of important information about a topic  **6:** a look back on past times or events

**review** (v.) **1:** to analyze something and assess it **2:** to think or talk about something again, in order to make changes or a decision about it; to take a second look (*The group reviewed all the applications one final time.*) **3:** to write an opinion about a book, movie, or product **4:** to visit and look at military groups **5:** to study something you have already learned

Peace or piece? See or sea? The English language is full of words that sound the same but that have different meanings and different spellings. Those words are called homophones. How do you ~~no~~ know ~~witch~~ which homophones ~~too~~ two to use?

Make sure you know the meanings of the homophones. Compare the spellings. Try to think of a way to remember the meanings and spellings. With practice, you will learn how to use homophones. Look at the example: *peace or piece?*

## What are the meanings?

peace (n.) a time of no war; a time of quiet or calm.
piece (n.) a part or bit of something.

## What is different about the spellings?

Both words have a long e sound, but the sound is spelled differently.

## Is there a way to remember the meanings or the spellings?

The word *piece* has the word *pie* in it. You can remember the spelling and meaning by thinking of a piece of pie.

## Give It a Try

**Read the meanings of the homophones.**
**Fill in the blanks with the correct homophone.**

**see (v.)** use your eyes / **sea (n.)** a body of water

1. The glare was so bright I couldn't _____.

2. The clouds were reflected in the _____ below.

3. _____ what I mean?

Think of a way to remember the meanings and spellings of *see* and *sea*.

Get practice using homophones by writing a sentence for each.

**Read the meanings of the homophones.**
**Fill in the blanks with the correct homophone.**

❶ **hear (v.)** use your ears / **here (n.)** the place where you are

A. There are no strangers _____ , only friends you have not met.

B. People may _____ your words, but they feel your attitude.

C. _____ they are!

❷ **plain (adj.)** ordinary; clear; simple / **plane (n.)** airplane

A. The best moments on a _____ are when you are asleep.

B. He told the _____ truth and nothing but the truth.

C. _____ everyday things are often the most important things.

❸ **sun (n.)** the star that gives Earth light and warmth / **son (n.)** a male child

A. She has a special place in her heart for her _____ .

B. Turn your face to the _____ ; then the shadows fall behind you.

C. The light of his life was his _____ .

❹ **our (adj.)** belonging to us / **hour (n.)** a chunk of time

A. During _____ darkest moments, we must focus to see the light.

B. A minute of thought is greater than an _____ of talk.

C. Let us put _____ minds together and see what life we can

make for _____ children.

❺ **whole (adj.)** complete, entire / **hole (n.)** an empty space in something

A. An eye for an eye only makes the _____ world blind.

B. The mouse that has only one _____ is quickly caught.

C. Faith is taking the first step even when you don't see the _____

staircase.

⑥ **right (adj.)** correct / **write (v.)** use written words or symbols to express meaning

   A. Trolls are nasty cowards who _____ nasty comments online.

   B. Put your feet in the _____ place and then stand firm.

   C. The time is always _____ to do what is _____ .

⑦ **waste (v.)** use for no purpose / **waist (n.)** part of the body

   A. _____ not, want not.

   B. Middle age is when your broad mind and narrow _____

   begin to change places.

   C. Don't _____ time, because time is what life is made up of.

⑧ **one (adj.)** a number / **won (v.)** past tense of win

   A. _____ good deed deserves another.

   B. They _____ the battle, but at what cost?

   C. Let insults go in _____ ear and out the other.

⑨ **steal (v.)** take what does not belong to you / **steel (n.)** a hard building material

   A. The dictator had a heart of _____ .

   B. Social media, like a thief, can _____ hours of your time.

   C. A lawyer with his briefcase can _____ more than a hundred men

   with guns.

⑩ **wait (v.)** do nothing until an expected event happens / **weight (n.)** what something weighs

   A. You need to pull your own _____ .

   B. Change will not come if we _____ for some other person or time.

   C. Opportunities are like sunrises—if you _____ too long, you miss them.

⑪ **break (v.)** put a stop to; go against / **brake (n.)** a thing that stops something

    A. Jealousy will put the _____ on developing trust.

    B. Sometimes you need to _____ the law to do the right thing.

    C. Research shows it takes 31 days to make or _____ a habit.

⑫ **week (n.)** seven days / **weak (adj.)** without strength

    A. Watching a boring movie feels like a _____ of Sundays.

    B. Ridicule is a _____ weapon when pointed at a strong mind.

    C. Man was made at the end of a _____ of work, when God was tired.

⑬ **heels (n.)** part of a foot or shoe / **heals (v.)** cures

    A. Laughter _____ .

    B. She dug her _____ in, refusing to change her mind.

    C. A person _____ by being able to tell their story—the whole story.

⑭ **meat (n.)** food from animals; main part / **meet (v.)** come together face to face

    A. Be kind, for everyone you _____ is fighting a hard battle.

    B. Laughter, love, and tears are the _____ and potatoes of life.

    C. If God did not want us to eat animals, then why did he make them of out _____ ?

⑮ **lesson (n.)** moral; time of instruction / **lessen (v.)** make less

    A. Being a parent is a _____ in self-sacrifice.

    B. No distance or time can _____ the friendship between two people

    who know each other's worth.

    C. Experience is a hard teacher—she gives the test first, the _____ afterward.

> **Which homophones in this unit are new for you? Practise by writing your own sentences. Think of interesting ways to remember their meanings and spellings.**

Many words are made up of root words and an affix. Knowing about parts of words can help you figure out the meanings of new words.

Each word below has a root word and an affix.
The root words are underlined. Circle the affixes.

semi<u>circle</u>          <u>end</u>less          kilo<u>metre</u>          <u>success</u>ful

Affixes that are added to the beginning of words are called *prefixes*.
Affixes that are added to the end of words are called *suffixes*.

## How can affixes help you figure out new words?

Prefixes and suffixes have their own meanings.
They change or add to the meaning of root words.

**Look at the examples below.**

*semi* = half

The Native Elders sat in a **semicircle** and listened to the storyteller.

You know the meaning of the root word *circle*. *Semicircle* means half a circle.

*kilo* = 1,000

The nuts were on sale, so the chef bought a **kilogram** of cashews.

You know the meaning of the root word *gram*. *Kilogram* means 1,000 grams.

## Give It a Try

**Circle the affix in each bolded word.**
**Read the meaning of each affix.**
**Discuss the meaning of the bolded words with your teacher.**

*less* = without

The trail seemed to be **endless** for the tired hikers.

*ful* = with / full of

Some people believe we will be **successful** in changing things for the better.

**Read the sentences.**
**Circle the prefix in each bolded word.**
**Choose the correct answer.**
**Use the meanings in the box to help you.**

| | |
|---|---|
| non = not | pre = before, in advance |
| over = too much | mis = bad(ly), wrong(ly) |

1. Don't **overuse** water. Which is an example of overusing water?

   A. taking a long shower    B. drinking a glass of water    C. spilling water

2. Don't **misuse** strong cleaners. How might you misuse a strong cleaner?

   A. clean the bathtub with it    B. wash your hands with it    C. store it

3. Try to find cleaning products that are **non-toxic**. Which material is toxic?

   A. baking soda    B. ammonia    C. lemon juice

4. **Prearrange** with friends to buy food in bulk. Why is that a good idea?

   A. It saves money.    B. Everyone eats the same food.    C. The food tastes better.

5. Avoid buying **prepackaged** food. Which food must be prepackaged?

   A. fish    B. apples    C. eggs

6. Do not **overheat** your home. Which can overheat your home?

   A. setting the temperature high    B. opening a window    C. turning on a fan

7. Don't buy things that are **non-essential**. Which is essential for life?

   A. a car    B. a TV    C. food

8. What if we **misjudge** the future effects of climate change? What will that lead to?

   A. a brighter future    B. being unprepared for change    C. breaking the law

**Read the paragraphs.**
**Circle the prefix in each bolded word.**
**Complete the sentences.**
**Use the meanings in the box to help you.**

> *multi = many*           *inter = between*
>
> *en = to cause to be*      *fore = before*

**1**  Water is life. We can live without food for three weeks, but we die without water after a few days. Water is also **multi-purpose**.

The writer is going to show us that water

A. can be multiplied.     B. has many uses.     C. is used in many places.

**2**  We use water in our homes and factories. We swim in it for fun, and we use it to produce energy. But mainly, water **enables** all things to live.

The writer is going to talk about how water

A. is able to live.     B. helps things live.     C. lives with all things.

**3**  Tiny animals, or organisms, live in water. They are so tiny that they are invisible. Humans and these tiny organisms **interact** every day. How does that happen?

The writer is going to explain how humans and organisms

A. compare with each other.     B. act in water.     C. have contact.

**4**  We need to think about how we use water. Do you leave the tap running while doing dishes? Do you take long showers? Saving water requires some **forethought** every time we use it.

The writer suggests that we think about our water use

A. before we use water.     B. while we use water.     C. after we use water.

**Complete the sentences using the bolded words and a suffix.**
**Use the meanings in the box to help you.**
**The first one is an example.**

> tion = state of, act of          er / or = one who does something
>
> en = to make, made of          able / ible = can be

**❶** Why would somebody want to **invent** an electric car?

What would lead to the _invention_ of the electric car?

**❷** We would use **less** fossil fuel if more people drove electric cars.

Driving electric cars would _____ our need for fossil fuels.

**❸** The lack of charging stations used to **restrict** people from using electric cars.

One _____ of using electric cars was the lack of charging stations.

**❹** When I **drive**, I do not want to stop all the time to recharge.

A _____ does not want to stop all the time to recharge.

**❺** Now, people can **depend** on electric cars more.

Now, electric cars are becoming more _____ .

**❻** Someday, I will **own** an electric car.

Someday, I will be the _____ of an electric car.

**❼** Electric cars are easier to **use** in warmer climates.

Electric cars are more _____ in warmer climates.

**❽** Arguments against electric cars will become **weak** as they improve.

Arguments against electric cars will _____ as they improve.

**Complete the sentences using the bolded words and a suffix.**
**Use the meanings in the box to help you.**
**The first one is an example.**

> ly = how something is done     ive = tending to be
> al = related to; like something     ment = act of, process of

1. Living in a tiny house means you need to **adjust** your lifestyle.
Living in a tiny house requires an _adjustment_.

2. Living in a small space means you need to **create** storage space.
Living in a small space means you have to be _____.

3. Some people furnish homes in a **cheap** way by going to garage sales.
Some people furnish homes _____ by going to garage sales.

4. Couples who live in a small space need to **cooperate**.
Couples who live in a small space need to be _____.

5. It's challenging to find enough space to **place** furniture in a tiny house.
The _____ of furniture in a tiny house is a challenge.

6. Living in a tiny home has more than one **benefit**.
Living in a tiny home is _____.

7. People live in a **modest** way by owning fewer things.
People live _____ by owning fewer things.

8. Tiny houses use fewer resources that come from **nature**, such as trees.
Tiny houses use fewer _____ resources such as trees.

In this book, you have learned different ways to figure out the meanings of new words and phrases. Read the following passages. Use what you have learned to answer the questions.

## Northern Dancer

*In 1964, Northern Dancer became the first Canadian horse to win the Kentucky Derby, a famous horserace in the U.S.*

Northern Dancer was the little horse that nobody wanted. His owner, E.P. Taylor, took Northern Dancer to sale after sale. Nobody wanted to pay $25,000 for the **stringy** little horse. Buyers wanted taller, more powerful horses. Taylor took the **yearling** back to his farm. That turned out to be the best thing that Taylor ever did.

Two years later, Northern Dancer won the Kentucky Derby. He finished the race in two minutes—and broke the track record. With that win, people began to **appreciate** the little horse with the big heart. Dancer was small, but he ran like the wind.

As a three-year-old, Dancer's wins came fast and furious. Canadians believed in the little horse and loved him. But other horseracing fans were **dubious**. Northern Dancer went on to win more major races. The little horse finally won the respect of even the strongest non-believers. He charmed the world.

**1**   Write a definition for *yearling*.

..............................................................................................................................................................................

**2**   Find and underline an antonym for *stringy*.

**3**   Find and underline the simile in paragraph 2. What is being compared?
Do you think the comparison is a good one? Why or why not?

**4**   Is the following statement true or false?
Find and underline a sentence to support your answer.

Dancer won only a few races over a long period of time. *True/False*

**5**   Which word is a synonym for dubious?   (a) believable   (b) doubtful   (c) respectful

**6**   Circle the best meaning for how *appreciate* is used in the passage.

---

**appreciate** (v.) **1:** be thankful for   **2:** put a high value on (*They appreciate a job that is well done.*): RESPECT   **3:** understand a situation fully (*I appreciate how much time you spent on this project.*) **4:** increase in price

---

39

## The King of Birds

*There are more chickens in the world than any other kind of bird.*
*Their history is long and rich.*

The chicken started in Asia as a wild bird called the Red Jungle Fowl. Along the way, the chicken has been **domesticated**, and people have used the tamed bird for different purposes.

The chicken found its way to Africa through trade. The first **evidence** of chickens in Africa is a drawing of a chicken on a 3,000-year-old pot. Writings of the time talk about the "royal bird" and the "bird that gives birth every day." People tamed chickens for **sacred** reasons, not food. For example, people in Egypt hung chicken eggs in their temples so that the gods would send floods. Floodwater left the soil rich and **fertile**. Fertile soil produced good crops.

For Romans, chickens were fortunetellers. Romans brought chickens with them to battles. They watched the chickens closely before a battle. They hoped the chickens would eat with **hearty** appetites. That meant the Romans would win the battle.

Today, chickens are food pre-wrapped in plastic and Styrofoam. That is **food for thought**.

❶ The title of the passage is a metaphor. What is being compared?
Do you think the comparison is a good one? Why or why not?

❷ a) Find and circle a synonym for *domesticated*.
b) Think of another common animal that is domesticated.

❸ Which word is a synonym for *sacred*?   (a) holy   (b) delicious   (c) old

❹ a) Which word is an antonym for *fertile*?   (a) wild   (b) flowering   (c) unproductive
b) Which word is an antonym for *hearty*?   (a) strange   (b) weak   (c) mighty

❺ What do you think the idiom *food for thought* means?

❻ Circle the best meaning for how *evidence* is used in the passage.

**evidence** (n.) **1:** fact that supports a belief  **2:** information used in a court of law  **3:** a sign of something (*His sweat was evidence of how hard he worked.*)

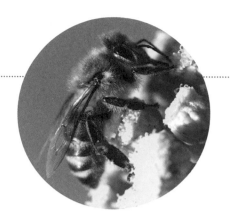

## Buzz Pollination

*More than 20,000 different kinds of bees exist in the world. All bees buzz when they fly, but bumblebees buzz even when they are not flying.*

Bees use their flying muscles to move their wings when they fly. The wings move fast and make a buzzing sound. But have you ever watched a bumblebee on a flower? The buzzing does not stop as the bumblebee crawls around and into the flower. Why this **incessant** buzzing? **Entomologists,** or bug scientists, have the answer. The bumblebee is busy buzz pollinating.

Bumblebees eat pollen produced by flowers. The pollen is stored in small **pods** inside the flower. Bumblebees brush up against the pods. They vibrate the flying muscles in their upper body, or **thorax**. The vibration shakes the pollen from inside the pods. It is the vibration that makes the buzzing sound.

Some pollen will settle like dust on the bumblebees. As the bumblebees fly from plant to plant, they move pollen from flower to flower. In other words, they **pollinate** the plants. And there you have it—buzz pollination.

① Find and underline meanings for these words:

A. entomologists   B. thorax   C. pollinate

② Find and circle a synonym for *incessant*.

③ a) Find and circle a simile in paragraph 3. What is being compared?
b) Which word best describes pollen? (i) dirty   (ii) powdery   (iii) slippery

④ Is the following statement true or false?
Find and underline a sentence to support your answer.

The buzzing sound comes from bees' muscles.   *True/False*

⑤ Circle the best meaning for how *pod* is used in the passage.

**pod** (n.) **1:** a separate part of a spaceship that can be detached
**2:** a small group of whales  **3:** the long thin part of a plant that holds seeds
**4:** the cocoon of a silkworm  **5:** the protective case around locust eggs

# Answer Key

## Unit 1: Context Clues

*Pages 6 - 7*
1. (d)
2. (c)
3. (a)
4. (d)
5. (c)
6. (d)
7. (a)

*Page 8*
Paragraph 1: (d)
Paragraph 2: *Escalated* means grew bigger or more intense.

*Page 9*
Paragraph 1: (b)
Paragraph 2: *Debris* means piles of loose material from rocks or plants.

*Page 10*
Paragraph 1: (d)
Paragraph 2: *Erosion* means the wearing away of the earth's surface by wind, water or glacial action.

## Unit 2: Metaphors and Similes

*Page 11*
1. Simile: Fog is compared to pea soup. The writer implies that the fog is so thick that you can't see through it.
2. Metaphor: Life is compared to a rollercoaster. The writer implies that life is full of ups and downs.
3. Simile: The show is compared to watching grass grow. Grass grows slowly. The writer implies that the show is slow and boring to watch.
4. Metaphor: The computer is compared to a dinosaur. The writer implies that the computer is very old and out of date.

*Pages 12 - 13*
1. a. The wind is compared to a knife.  b. (ii)
2. a. The ocean is compared to boiling water.  b. (iv)
3. a. Ideas are compared to a storm.  b. (i)
4. a. Memories are compared to a fog.
5. a. Her daughter is compared to sunshine.
6. a. The flooding river is compared to a mouth.

*Page 14*
1. (b)
2. (a)
3. (c)
4. (a)
5. (c)

*Pages 15 - 16*
1. a. The sun is compared to warm toast. b. (ii)
2. a. Clouds are compared to cotton candy. b. (i)
3. a. Summer days are compared to a wet blanket.  b. (iii)
4. a. Frosty sidewalks are compared to ice.
5. a. Shoveling is compared to eating dirt.
6. a. The movement of wind is compared to a kitten.

*Page 17*

Student choices will vary. Accept any answer that is supported with a good reason.

## Unit 3: Idioms

*Pages 19 - 21*

❶ (d)
❷ (d)
❸ (d)
❹ (b)
❺ (b)
❻ (d)
❼ (a)
❽ (a)
❾ (c)

*Pages 22-23*

❶ *Snowed under* means having too much to do.
❷ *Go the extra mile* means doing more than is expected of you.
❸ *Bite off more than you can chew* means trying to do more than you are able.
❹ *Calling the shots* means making decisions that will affect a situation.
❺ *Burn bridges* means destroying all chances of going back to a situation.
❻ *Keep your head down* means avoiding trouble by minding your own business.

## Unit 4: Dictionary

*Page 24:*

❶ 4
❷ noun (n.)
❸ c.
❹ much force or strength

*Page 25:*

❶ verb
❷ 3
❸ 5
❹ 3
❺ adjective (adj.)
❻ Student answers will vary.
❼ *Valid* is an adjective. Adjectives do not have a plural form.

*Page 26:*

❷ (n. 5)
❸ (n. 4)
❹ (v. 2)
❺ (n. 2)
❻ (n. 3)
❼ (n. 1)
❽ (n. 2)

*Page 27:*

❷ (v. 3)
❸ (v. 4)
❹ (v. 6)
❺ (v. 2)
❻ (v. 5)
❼ (n.)
❽ (adj. 2)
❾ (adj. 1)
❿ (v. 1)

*Page 28:*

❷ (v. 5)

❸ (n. 6)

❹ (v. 4)

❺ (v. 2)

❻ (n. 3)

❼ (n. 5)

❽ (v. 1)

❾ (v. 3)

❿ (n. 2)

# Unit 5: Homophones

*Page 29:*

❶ see

❷ sea

❸ See

*Pages 30 – 32\**

❶ (a) here  (b) hear  (c) Here

❷ (a) plane  (b) plain  (c) Plain

❸ (a) son  (b) sun  (c) son

❹ (a) our  (b) hour  (c) our, our

❺ (a) whole  (b) hole  (c) whole

❻ (a) write  (b) right  (c) right, right

❼ (a) Waste  (b) waist  (c) waste

❽ (a) One  (b) won  (c) one

❾ (a) steel  (b) steal  (c) steal

❿ (a) weight  (b) wait  (c) wait

⓫ (a) brake  (b) break  (c) break

⓬ (a) week  (b) weak  (c) week

⓭ (a) heals  (b) heels  (c) heals

⓮ (a) meet  (b) meat  (c) meat

⓯ (a) lesson  (b) lessen  (c) lesson

# Unit 6: Affixes

*Page 34*

❶ (a)

❷ (b)

❸ (b)

❹ (a)

❺ (c)

❻ (a)

❼ (c)

❽ (b)

*Page 35*

❶ (b)

❷ (b)

❸ (c)

❹ (a)

*Page 36*

❷ lessen

❸ restriction

❹ driver

❺ dependable

❻ owner

❼ useable

❽ weaken

*Page 37*

❷ creative

❸ Cheaply

❹ cooperative

❺ placement

❻ beneficial

❼ modestly

❽ natural

# Unit 7: Summary

## Page 39: Northern Dancer

1. a horse that is one year old
2. powerful
3. he ran like the wind / Dancer's fast speed is being compared to wind.
4. False: As a three-year-old, Dancer's wins came fast and furious.
5. (b)
6. Definition 2

## Page 41: The King of Birds

1. Chickens are being compared to kings.
2. a. tamed  b. Possible answers: horses, cows, dogs
3. (a)
4. a. (c)  b. (b)
5. something to think about
6. Definition 3

## Page 43: Buzz Pollination

1. a. bug scientists  b. upper body
   c. move pollen from flower to flower
2. does not stop
3. a. Some pollen will settle like dust /
   The way pollen covers the bumblebee is compared to how dust covers something.
   b. (ii)
4. True: It is the vibration that makes the buzzing sound.
5. Definition 3

*Quotes on pages 29-30
1. (a) W.B. Yeats  (b) John C. Maxwell
3. (b) unknown
4. (a) Aristotle  (b) John C. Maxwell
   (c) Sitting Bull
5. (a) Martin Luther King Jr.
   (b) George Herbert  (c) Mahatma Gandhi
6. (b) Tom Wilson  (c) Martin Luther King Jr.
7. (b) E. Joseph Crossman  (c) Bruce Lee
9. (c) Mario Puzo
10. (b) Barack Obama  (c) William Arthur Ward
12. (b) Martin Farquhar Tupper  (c) Mark Twain
13. (c) Clarissa Pinkola Estes
14. (b) Philo  (c) John Cleese
15. (b) Robert Southey  (c) Vernon Law